THE KATHLEEN PARTRIDGE SERIES

Kathleen Partridge's Book of Flowers
Kathleen Partridge's Book of Friendship
Kathleen Partridge's Book of Golden Thoughts
Kathleen Partridge's Book of Tranquil Moments
Kathleen Partridge's Book of Faith
Kathleen Partridge's Book of Happiness
Kathleen Partridge's Book of Seasons
Kathleen Partridge's Book of Hope

First published in Great Britain in 1997 by
Jarrold Publishing Ltd
Whitefriars, Norwich NR3 1TR

Designed and produced by Visual Image, Craigend, Brimley Hill,
Churchstanton, Taunton, Somerset TA3 7QH

Illustrations by Jane Watkins

Edited by Donald Greig

ISBN 0-7117-0969-6

Copyright © Jarrold Publishing 1997

Printed by Proost, Belgium 1/97

Kathleen Partridge's
BOOK OF

Seasons

Kathleen Partridge

Spring

In Spring, the loveliest of sights
Anemones and aconites,
Down woodland ways, the first sweet
flowers
To tell the beauty of the hours.

And when the aconite is over
There will be crocus in the clover,
Mauve and yellow, green and gold
Beneath the trees grown wise and old.

No car could travel down those lanes
Where Spring begins and Winter wanes,
This is the path by footsteps trod
The haven of a gracious God.

So sings the heart this golden morn
The first song that was ever born,
For fragrant air and spring delights
Anemones and aconites.

Robbing the Spring

Though not a thief, yet I should like to
steal the zest of Spring,
To borrow all her harmony of light
and colouring.

To copy in my home the sun and
shadows that she blends
And take her joy of living to distribute
to my friends.

I'd like no one perfume, but all the
fragrance out of doors
To sprinkle in my rooms and wash my
cupboards and my floors.

I'd like her calm efficiency
about my little toil,
The bravery with which she starts again
when projects spoil.

I watch the world with wonder, every cloud
and growing thing,
And I try to take a pattern from the
wisdom of the spring.

Easter

Come Easter! With your golden key
Unlock the winter's mystery;
Such treasures wait upon your will,
Reveal the golden daffodil,
Unlock the tulip's hard green case
And set the jonquil in her place.

For Spring is dancing at your side,
And when the door is open wide,
We shall discover hope anew
Where frosts of grief have changed to
dew.

And we shall know in joy sublime
That God was with us all the time,
Guiding us through frost and storm
To Easter days and sunshine warm.

When God Smiles

Stamen by stamen and leaf by leaf
The earth grows lovely beyond belief,
Blade after blade the grass renews
The lush green colour of wayside views.

Primrose by primrose the air grows sweet
Mixing and making the Spring complete,
Sunbeam by sunbeam for miles and miles
The world grows fairer because God smiles.

Summer

JULY 2001

If one sweet summer day
Can blend the sound and scent together
To be remembered always
As the ideal summer weather.

If just one rose is perfect
Be it yellow, be it white,
Then shall it make a memory
To carry through the night.

And we shall lift our eyes
To find serenity anew
In the heavenly mingling
Of the silver with the blue.

And all the goodness of the earth
Shall shine in glad array
As if a lifetime's loveliness
Lived in one summer's day.

Roses

Though days are sunny, sweet and clear,
I never feel that summer's here
Until the roses open wide,
Revealing perfumed hearts inside.

Though heat waves cannot come too soon,
I never quite believe in June
Until the hazy morning shows
The dew upon a crimson rose.

For roses are the summer's dream,
In pink or scarlet, white or cream;
I doubt that summer comes at all
Until the rambler climbs the wall.

Midsummer Day

*I must hurry, I must hurry, for the early
morning light
Has broken through my window and
the roses are in sight;
Green leaves have caught the sunbeams
and the dew is on the grass. . .
A petal may have fallen if I linger 'ere I
pass.*

*I must not miss a moment, summer goes
too swiftly by,
One day is still the lifetime of a brilliant
butterfly;
Fair earth, sweet fragrant summer, full of
song and golden rays,
Wait for me to count your treasures, wait
for me to add my praise.*

Opening Time

Waterlilies on a lake
What a restful sight they make!
Flat the leaves that quiver slightly
Where the wagtails tread so lightly.

Hawks and herons come and go
Where the peaceful waters flow,
When foxgloves toll for time and tide
The lilies close at eventide.

Autumn

2012

Mellow weather, tweeds and heather
Golden grows the gorse,
Beech leaves turning, creeper burning
Grass becoming coarse.

Fields of stubble, brooks that bubble
Lanes with rainbow ruts,
Hedges looped with blackberries
And bushes decked with nuts.

Hips and haws by scores and scores
And honey from the bees,
Mushrooms in the dewy dell
And moss beneath trees.

A world of wealth and wonder
Where the leaves dance as they fall
And all we lack is just the time
To go and see it all.

The Scent of Autumn

Autumn is scented with fruit that has fallen
The burning of bonfires and turning of loam,
Mists in the morning, so faintly refreshing
And smoke from the chimneys that beckon me
home.

Late flowering roses distil their sweet perfume
Blending along with the thyme and the mint,
But the smell of nasturtiums, this flower of the
Autumn
Is rioting colour that blooms without stint.

Autumn Sunshine

A shower of autumn sunbeams
Golden flecks among the brown,
Mild days and mellow moments
Fashion earth a golden gown.

Capture it and keep it
For a memory in your mind,
Look at it and love it
Ere the year leaves it behind.

And one day you will remember
How your eyes became awake
To a shower of autumn sunbeams
That were falling in a lake.

Between Seasons

Autumn and winter are like old friends meeting,
Who haven't been able to visit before,
They each bring a gift for the love of the other
And wrap it in silver outside the front door.

The gold leaves of autumn are trembling with winter,
The grass by the wayside is spangled with frost,
Old times and old pleasures have now been
exchanged
And the new is retold by the leaves twirled and
tossed.

Winter and autumn are sharing their memories,
Linked by the sun and the wind – arm in arm;
Soon they will part and fulfil lonely duties,
But together they bring the world beauty and charm.

Winter

The garden sleeps and dreams
Now that the season's work is ended,
A sense of peace and idleness
Has all the world befriended.

The hardy blossoms that are left
Look tattered and forlorn,
Only the berries shine for joy
And wait for Christmas morn.

And so there is serenity
About the garden dreaming,
Duty is fulfilled
There is no reason now for scheming.

The last tired leaf relaxing
Finds it only has to fall
And earth waits in her wisdom
With a resting place for all.

November Smiles

There'll be heather on the hillside
when the mist has rolled away,
There'll be lovely purple patches for
the beauty of the day;
November, damp and chilly in
tradition of the past,
Shows an ugly countenance that has
to smile at last.

And when she smiles there's heather,
white and blue and amethyst,
Shining on the hillside with the
passing of the mist;
Proving that the world can find an
answer to our dreams –
Though trouble comes, it isn't quite as
gloomy as it seems.

Winter Friend

Some call it 'poison ivy'
But it is a winter friend
And stays when red hot pokers fade
And tiger lilies end.

Constant and contented
On the garden wall it grows
Sheltering the birds
From every stormy wind that blows.

A Garland to Remember

We do not look for primroses in winter,
Nor yearn for blossoms when the trees are bare,
We learn to know the symbols of the seasons
And manage with the blessings that are there.

Nor should we waste our longings on the hopeless,
Nor yearn for things we cannot now afford,
For every circumstance has some advantage,
Just as each season brings its own reward.

Accept life as it comes, now chill, now sunny,
And gather some small garland to remember,
Not seeking holly berries in the summer,
Nor longing for the lilac in November.